12 INCREDIBLE FACTS ABOUT THE
DROPPING OF THE ATOMIC BOMBS

by Angie Smibert

12
STORY
LIBRARY

www.12StoryLibrary.com

12-Story Library is an imprint of Peterson Publishing Company and Press Room Editions.

Produced for 12-Story Library by Red Line Editorial

Photographs ©: Photographs ©: US Air Force/AP Images, cover, 1; Orren Jack Turner/Library of Congress, 4; Bettmann/Corbis, 5, 18, 21, 28, 29; US Navy/Library of Congress, 6; Los Alamos Laboratory/AP Images, 8; Horace Cort/AP Images, 9; AP Images, 11, 12, 13, 23, 24, 25; Library of Congress, 14; Cpl John W. Saunders/US Marine Corps History Division, 15; US Army/Library of Congress, 16; US Army/AP Images, 19; Clover/AP Images, 22; TommL/ iStockphoto, 26; Pierre Yu/iStock/Thinkstock, 27

ISBN
978-1-63235-129-6 (hardcover)
978-1-63235-172-2 (paperback)
978-1-62143-224-1 (hosted ebook)

Library of Congress Control Number: 2015933984

Printed in the United States of America
Mankato, MN
June, 2015

STORY
LIBRARY

Go beyond the book. Get free, up-to-date content on this topic at 12StoryLibrary.com.

0 1021 0401986 8

TABLE OF CONTENTS

EINSTEIN WARNS OF ATOMIC BOMBS

On August 2, 1939, Albert Einstein signed a historic letter. It was addressed to President Franklin Delano Roosevelt. Einstein was a famous physicist. He'd moved from Germany to the United States in 1933. That was just before the Nazi Party came to power.

In December 1938, German physicists reported they had split a uranium atom. Other scientists who had fled Europe brought this discovery to Einstein's attention. Splitting a uranium atom released a lot of energy. They worried this technology could be used to create a deadly bomb.

Einstein was already well known in the United States. The other scientists urged Einstein to contact the president. They thought Roosevelt might listen to him. One of those scientists, Leo Szilard, drafted a letter for Einstein. In it, he told the president that the Germans' research could create extremely powerful bombs.

On October 11, 1939, Roosevelt received Einstein's letter. He

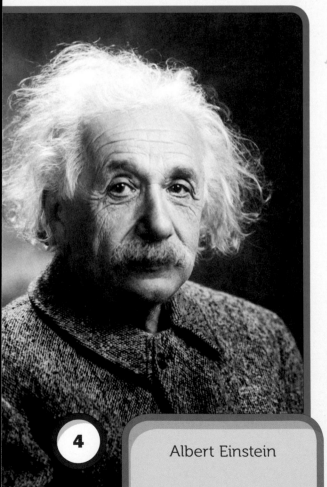

Albert Einstein

Leo Szilard wrote a letter for President Roosevelt.

1939
Year of the first meeting of the Advisory Committee on Uranium.

- Einstein was a famous scientist.
- Einstein signed a letter to President Roosevelt.
- The letter told Roosevelt about German research with uranium that might result in a powerful type of bomb.
- Roosevelt formed a committee to investigate making an atomic bomb.

immediately took action. Roosevelt formed the Advisory Committee on Uranium. This was one of the first steps that led to developing the atomic bomb.

JAPANESE ATTACK DRAWS THE UNITED STATES INTO WAR

Early Sunday morning, December 7, 1941, the Japanese military attacked Pearl Harbor, Hawaii. The harbor was the home of the US Navy's Pacific Fleet. Japanese planes destroyed hundreds of US aircraft parked on the runways.

Other Japanese fighters and bombers attacked battleships in the harbor. Many US ships were sunk. The attack lasted only

The USS *Arizona* burns during the attack on Pearl Harbor.

829

Number of days between the start of World War II and the attack on Pearl Harbor.

THINK ABOUT IT

What events led up to the United States entering World War II? Find three examples on these pages to illustrate your answer.

- Japan attacked Pearl Harbor, Hawaii, on December 7, 1941.
- The attack drew the United States into World War II.
- Japan was allied with Germany and Italy.

two hours, but 2,500 American lives were lost.

The attack on Pearl Harbor brought a war that had been raging around the world to Americans' doorsteps. For much of the world, the war had started years earlier. On September 1, 1939, German tanks rolled into Poland. The next day, Great Britain and France declared war on Germany. While Germany's ally Japan tried to conquer China and other East Asian countries, Germany marched through Europe.

The United States had hoped to stay out of the war. But it wanted to help its allies too. In the summer of 1941, the United States, along with its allies Great Britain and the Netherlands, refused to sell oil to Japan. In response, Japan planned the secret attack on Pearl Harbor.

After Pearl Harbor, more Americans felt it was necessary to join the war. President Roosevelt declared war on Japan on December 8, 1941. Japan's allies—Germany and Italy— declared war on the United States. Japan, Germany, Italy, and several smaller countries made up the Axis Powers. The United States joined Great Britain, France, the Soviet Union, China, and a few others to form the Allied Powers. As the United States readied its troops for a war across the ocean, it also worked on developing new war weapons.

SECRET CITIES FORM TO DEVELOP ATOMIC BOMBS

3

In August 1942, the Manhattan District of the Army Corps of Engineers was given an important job. Its aim was to develop and build atomic bombs. But everything had to be done in secret. The mission was code-named the Manhattan Project.

The Manhattan Project built secret cities for its laboratories and factories across the country. These places would research and develop atomic bombs. Scientists and workers would live there with their families. Some of the cities were so secret that they didn't appear on maps.

The first site was an abandoned boys' school in the desert north of Santa Fe, New Mexico. It was named Los Alamos Laboratory. The Manhattan Project also built two other secret cities: Oak Ridge, Tennessee, and Hanford, Washington. Both had huge factories for making fuel for the bombs.

More than 125,000 people were employed at these three cities alone. Employees were issued badges and driver's licenses without names. They were forbidden to talk about their work with even their families.

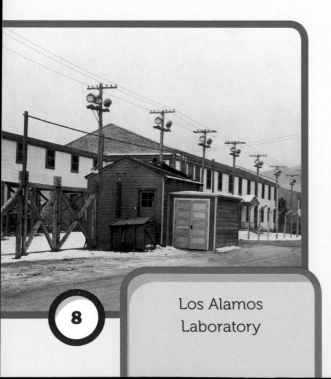

Los Alamos Laboratory

16

Distance, in miles (26 km), from Los Alamos to the nearest populated town.

- During World War II, the US built secret research labs and production plants all over the country.
- The code name for this effort was the Manhattan Project.
- The three largest and most secret cities were Los Alamos, Oak Ridge, and Hanford.

SPLITTING AN ATOM

In December 1942, Nobel Prize–winning physicist Enrico Fermi and his team at the University of Chicago produced the first controlled nuclear chain reaction. That is, his group split the atom without causing a deadly explosion. When controlled, a chain reaction could produce huge amounts of energy. This made the atomic bomb and nuclear energy possible.

Workers leaving the atomic bomb production plant in Oak Ridge, Tennessee, at the end of the day.

FIRST ATOMIC BOMB VAPORIZES TEST TOWER

At 5:30 a.m. on July 16, 1945, a burst of white light blanked out the sky over a remote corner of the desert near Alamogordo, New Mexico. Wearing dark goggles, observers from Los Alamos and the military watched from bunkers more than five miles (8 km) from the test tower.

This was the Trinity Test. It was the first explosion of an atomic bomb. The white light faded quickly into a huge orange and yellow fireball. Seconds later a blast wave tore across the desert. It knocked over observers and heavy equipment miles away. The heat vaporized the steel test tower. It turned the surrounding sand into green glass shards. An immense mushroom-shaped cloud rose over the test site.

The Trinity Test was a key moment. It proved that the plutonium-based bomb, nicknamed "Fat Man," worked. Los Alamos scientists were already confident that the uranium-based bomb, "Little Boy," would work.

2,400
Length, in feet (732 m), of the crater created by the Trinity Test.

- On July 16, 1945, the Manhattan Project detonated a nuclear bomb.
- The secret test site was a remote corner of Alamogordo, New Mexico.
- The test was called Trinity.
- The plutonium-based bomb worked.

Scientists and workers raise the first atomic bomb into the test tower.

"IT WORKED," OPPENHEIMER SAYS

One of those people anxiously watching the Trinity Test was Dr. Robert Oppenheimer. He was the scientific director of the Manhattan Project. Working at Los Alamos Laboratory, Oppenheimer was under a lot of pressure. The military wanted an atomic bomb quickly. He barely breathed as he watched the seconds tick by. When the Trinity Test announcer cried "Now!" the bomb lit up the sky. Oppenheimer relaxed. "It worked," he simply said.

Much later, Oppenheimer admitted that he was unnerved at that moment. Inspired by the Bhagavad Gita, the Hindu scripture, he thought of the following lines, "I am become

After the test, General Leslie R. Groves (right) and Oppenheimer examine the area where the test tower once stood.

death, the destroyer of worlds." He had just become the "father of the atomic bomb."

Before the Manhattan Project, Oppenheimer was already a well-known physicist. He earned a PhD in theoretical physics from Göttingen University in Germany in 1927. By 1929, he was a researcher and professor at the University of California, Berkeley, and the California Institute of Technology. In 1942, General Leslie R. Groves, director of the Manhattan Project, selected Oppenheimer to manage its the scientific aspects.

3,000
Number of people working for Oppenheimer at Los Alamos.

- Oppenheimer was a US physicist.
- In 1942, he became the scientific director of the Manhattan Project.
- He is known as the "father of the atomic bomb."

Dr. Robert Oppenheimer

THINK ABOUT IT

Imagine you are Oppenheimer witnessing the successful atomic bomb test. How would you feel knowing that the bomb worked?

TRUMAN MAKES A BIG DECISION

On April 12, 1945, President Franklin Delano Roosevelt died unexpectedly. His vice president, Harry S. Truman, was sworn in as president the next day. That day, Secretary of War Henry Stimson told Truman about the existence of a powerful new weapon. Two weeks later, Stimson and General Groves briefed Truman about the Manhattan Project. They told him that the first atomic bomb would be ready to test in several months.

Germany surrendered on May 8, 1945. The United States and its allies had won the war in Europe. But Japan continued to fight. Now Truman faced a difficult decision. Should he use the atomic bomb to end the war with Japan?

US bombers were already regularly striking Japanese cities. A firebomb raid on Tokyo in March 1945 had killed 100,000 people. But Japan fought on. A full-scale attack by troops was planned for November 1945. However, many feared this might cost millions of lives. In May 1945 alone, the United States had lost 75,000 men in combat on the

President
Harry S. Truman

Japanese islands of Iwo Jima and Okinawa.

Truman's advisors recommended dropping the atomic bomb to convince Japan to surrender. On July 26, 1945, the Allies issued the Potsdam Declaration to Japan. It called for the unconditional surrender of Japan's military. When Japan rejected it, Truman approved the use of atomic bombs as soon as they were ready.

2 million

Number of Japanese soldiers still guarding Japan before the atomic bombs were dropped.

- Truman became president after Roosevelt died.
- Truman faced the hard decision of whether to use the atomic bomb to end the war.
- In July 1945, Truman ordered the atomic bombs to be used as soon as they were ready.

Marines fire on the enemy in Okinawa, Japan.

7

"LITTLE BOY" DESTROYS TWO-THIRDS OF HIROSHIMA

On the morning of August 6, 1945, a B-29 plane named the *Enola Gay* took off from a US military base on Tinian Island, a small island in the Western Pacific Ocean. The *Enola Gay* carried a 10-foot-long

(3-m) atomic bomb. The bomb was called "Little Boy." Its target was Hiroshima, Japan.

At 8:15 a.m., the *Enola Gay* dropped "Little Boy" over Hiroshima. Forty-

Hiroshima after the atomic bomb was dropped

80,000

Estimated number of people killed instantly when the atomic bomb was dropped on Hiroshima.

- On August 6, 1945, the United States dropped the first atomic bomb.
- Its target was Hiroshima, Japan.
- Two-thirds of the city was destroyed.

ENOLA GAY

The *Enola Gay* was one of 15 B-29 Superfortress bomber planes. These were planes that had been modified to carry an atomic bomb. Pilot Colonel Paul Tibbets named the plane after his mother. His squadron was stationed on Tinian Island.

three seconds later the bomb detonated 1,900 feet (579 m) above the city. Below, the city was bustling with life on a sunny Monday morning. Hundreds of soldiers were training on the ground. People were biking or walking to work. Children were in school.

The people closest to the hypocenter, or ground zero, died instantly. Some were vaporized by the intense heat. Temperatures at the hypocenter reached up to 122 million degrees Fahrenheit (50 million °C). The blast wave that followed knocked people off their feet. It collapsed buildings. Within minutes, 90 percent of the people within a half mile (0.8 km) of ground zero were dead.

Nearly every structure within a mile (1.6 km) of the hypocenter was destroyed. Even within three miles (4.8 km), buildings were severely damaged. As these structures burned, individual fires merged. They formed an immense firestorm. It engulfed 4.4 square miles (7 square km) of Hiroshima. The fire killed almost everyone within that area who had survived the bomb. After 15 minutes, a radioactive "black rain" began to fall. This stained people's skin and clothing. It contaminated food and water.

8

NAGASAKI IS NOT THE PRIMARY TARGET

In the early hours of August 9, 1945, another B-29 took off from Tinian Island. This plane—named *Bockscar*—carried "Fat Man." This was the much more powerful plutonium-fueled bomb. The plane's original destination was Kokura. That city produced military weapons. However, the sky over the target was not clear enough for the crew to drop the bomb accurately. So the pilot flew to the secondary target: Nagasaki. It was an important shipbuilding center and port.

At 11:02 a.m., "Fat Man" detonated 1,650 feet (503 m) over Nagasaki. The bomb was more powerful than the one dropped on Hiroshima. But the damage to the city wasn't as great. The hills surrounding the city

A plutonium-fueled bomb, like "Fat Man"

may have contained some of the blast from the explosion. Only the center of the city was completely destroyed. Still, an estimated 40,000 people were killed. Approximately a third of the city was destroyed.

60,000

Height, in feet (18,288 m), of the mushroom cloud caused by "Fat Man."

- On August 9, 1945, the United States dropped the second atomic bomb on Nagasaki.
- The initial target was Kokura.
- This bomb was more powerful than the one dropped on Hiroshima.
- The inner core of Nagasaki was destroyed.

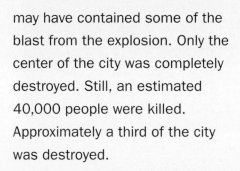

The inside of a torpedo factory in Nagasaki after the atomic bomb was dropped

9

NUCLEAR BLAST BURNS SHADOWS INTO THE GROUND

Witnesses in both Hiroshima and Nagasaki reported seeing an intense white light in the first seconds of the explosion. The flash was so intense it burned dark patterns from clothing into the wearer's skin. The light also burned shadows of people and objects onto walls and concrete. In some cases, the heat vaporized the person, leaving only his or her shadow. The searing heat and light from the initial nuclear explosion are a form of radiation. It is called thermal radiation.

Several days after the bombings, some survivors began to die of a mysterious illness. It was caused by another form of radiation called ionizing radiation. The patients had severe radiation sickness. Its symptoms include nausea, diarrhea, vomiting, headache, fever, hair loss, and seizures. The combined effect of thermal and ionizing radiation was lethal for people within approximately one mile (1.6 km) of ground zero. A few months after the bombings, it was estimated that 90,000 to 166,000 people total

IONIZING RADIATION

Ionizing radiation is energy given off by unstable atoms—like those used in nuclear weapons. Before August 1945, the effect of ionizing radiation on humans wasn't well understood. It can damage living cells. At a very high dose over a short period of time, ionizing radiation can cause radiation sickness.

70

Percentage of Hiroshima victims who suffered from more than one type of injury.

- Some survivors began to die of a mysterious illness days after the bombings.
- This illness turned out to be radiation sickness.
- Other survivors developed cancer years after the attack.

had died in Hiroshima as result of the bomb. In Nagasaki, 60,000 to 80,000 people died in that same period.

Those survivors who didn't suffer radiation sickness faced long-term effects. Exposure to large doses of radiation can cause cancer and birth defects. The most deadly form of cancer these survivors faced was leukemia. Two years after Hiroshima and Nagasaki, some survivors—particularly children—developed leukemia. Other cancers took longer to appear.

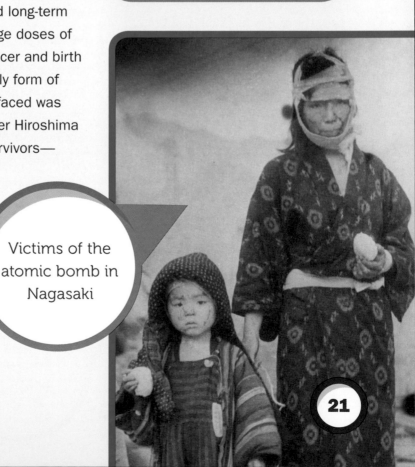

Victims of the atomic bomb in Nagasaki

21

JAPAN SURRENDERS A DAY AFTER NAGASAKI BOMBING

After Hiroshima was bombed, the Japanese government met to decide what to do next. Emperor Hirohito, who had little government power, urged the Imperial Council to end the war. However, the army and navy leaders wanted to hold out. They hoped the Soviet Union would help Japan get a better peace settlement with the United States. But on August 8, the Soviet Union declared war on Japan. The next day, the United States bombed Nagasaki.

The Imperial Council voted again on whether or not to surrender. The vote was tied. Emperor Hirohito broke the tie in favor of surrender.

On August 10, Japan accepted the Potsdam Declaration. In a radio broadcast to the people of Japan, Emperor Hirohito announced the surrender. One of the reasons he gave was that the enemy had used "a new and most cruel bomb." The formal surrender was made aboard the USS *Missouri* on September 2, 1945.

Emperor Hirohito

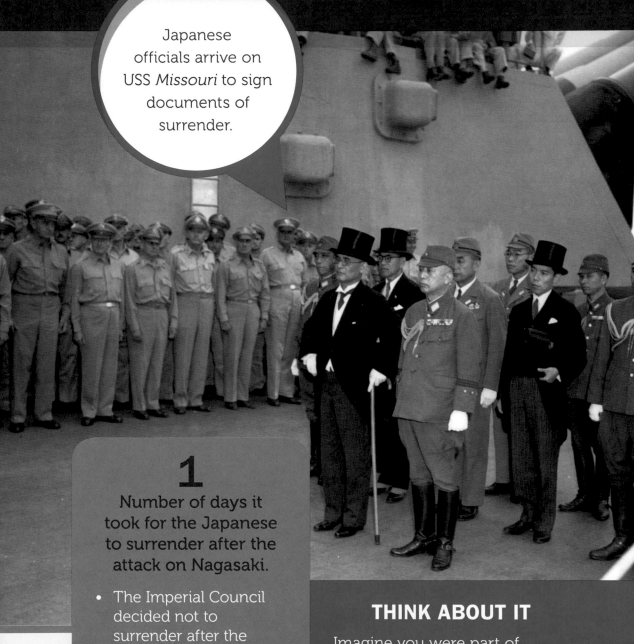

Japanese officials arrive on USS *Missouri* to sign documents of surrender.

1

Number of days it took for the Japanese to surrender after the attack on Nagasaki.

- The Imperial Council decided not to surrender after the atomic bomb was dropped on Hiroshima.
- Japan officially surrendered on September 2, 1945.
- Emperor Hirohito cited the atomic bombs as a reason for surrender in his radio address.

THINK ABOUT IT

Imagine you were part of Japan's Imperial Council. Would you vote to surrender? Write down three reasons to support your vote.

AN "IRON CURTAIN" DIVIDES EUROPE

On March 5, 1946, former British Prime Minister Winston Churchill declared that an "iron curtain" had fallen across Europe. After World War II, the Soviet Union began setting up communist governments in many countries in Eastern Europe. Churchill's "iron curtain" was the invisible barrier between communist and noncommunist countries. Churchill declared that there was a growing cold war between the countries. In a cold war, the two

Churchill gives his "Iron Curtain" speech.

CUBAN MISSILE CRISIS

For 13 days in October 1962, the United States and Soviet Union stood on the brink of nuclear war. The Soviet Union had nuclear missiles in Cuba, 90 miles (145 km) off the coast of Florida. When this was discovered, the United States blockaded Cuba with naval vessels. President John F. Kennedy threatened to remove the Soviet missiles by force. After a tense showdown, the Soviet Union agreed to remove the missiles if the United States promised not to invade Cuba.

Anti-aircraft missiles are showcased in a Soviet military parade.

sides use everything but open warfare to compete for power. The threat of nuclear weapons would play a key role in this new type of war.

After World War II, the Cold War between the United States and the Soviet Union increased. The United States refused to tell other countries how it built nuclear weapons. The

45

Approximate number of years the Cold War lasted.

- Churchill's speech drew attention to the growing Cold War.
- Atomic weapons would be a focal point of the Cold War.

Soviet Union raced to build its own nuclear weapons. It succeeded in detonating its first atomic bomb in 1949.

In 1951, the United States tested the hydrogen bomb. It was 450 times more powerful than "Fat Man." The Soviet Union followed with its own hydrogen bomb four years later. Throughout the 1950s and 1960s, both sides of the Cold War raced to build more and more powerful nuclear weapons and missiles. Neither one wanted to be at the mercy of other. Each side had the ability to destroy the other.

12

LIMITATION IS PLACED ON NUCLEAR WEAPONS

The destruction caused by the atomic bombs left a legacy. It made people realize how dangerous nuclear weapons could be. The Cold War made people worried that a nuclear war was possible. They started to think about ways to prevent the use of nuclear weapons.

On August 5, 1963, the United States, Soviet Union, and Great Britain signed the Limited Test Ban Treaty. This treaty banned the testing of nuclear weapons in the atmosphere, space, and underwater. Underground testing was still allowed.

The treaty began an era of nuclear arms talks and more treaties. In 1968, the Nuclear Non-Proliferation Treaty limited nuclear weapons to the countries that had already developed them. No new nuclear weapons could be created. The United States, the Soviet Union,

Hiroshima Peace Memorial

Genbaku Dome

China, Great Britain, France, and 59 other countries all eventually signed this treaty.

The dropping of the atomic bombs shaped much of US history during the Cold War—and beyond. The new weapons left a wake of fear. But they also raised awareness about the dangers of radiation. And they inspired some people to support more peaceful solutions to world conflicts.

3

Number of countries that signed the Limited Test Ban Treaty on August 5, 1963.

- The United States, Great Britain, and the Soviet Union signed a treaty to limit testing nuclear weapons.
- In 1968, the Nuclear Non-Proliferation Treaty banned the production of new nuclear weapons.

GENBAKU DOME

The Genbaku Dome was the only building in Hiroshima near the hypocenter to survive the atomic bomb. Today, it is part of Hiroshima Peace Memorial Park. It is a symbol of peace and disarmament. The Hiroshima Peace Flame has burned there since 1964.

12 KEY DATES

December 1938
German scientists split the atom.

August 2, 1939
Einstein signs a letter to President Roosevelt.

December 7, 1941
Japan attacks Pearl Harbor, Hawaii.

December 8, 1941
The United States declares war on Japan.

August 1942
The Manhattan Project is formed.

July 16, 1945
The first atomic bomb is exploded during the Trinity Test.

August 6, 1945
The United States drops an atomic bomb on Hiroshima, Japan.

August 9, 1945
The United States drops an atomic bomb on Nagasaki, Japan.

September 2, 1945
Japan officially surrenders aboard the USS *Missouri*.

March 5, 1946
Churchill makes his "Iron Curtain" speech.

August 5, 1963
The Limited Nuclear Test Ban Treaty is signed.

July 1, 1968
The United States, the Soviet Union, and many other countries sign the Nuclear Non-Proliferation Treaty.

GLOSSARY

atom
The smallest part of an element that still has the properties of the element.

blockade
The act of blocking goods or people from entering or leaving a country.

detonate
To explode.

firestorm
A powerful and destructive fire.

ground zero
The center of a nuclear explosion. See *hypocenter*.

hypocenter
The point on the earth's surface directly below the center of a nuclear bomb explosion.

lethal
Able to cause death.

plutonium
A radioactive metallic element.

radiation
The process of giving off energy in the form of waves or particles.

radioactive
A substance that gives off radiation.

uranium
A heavy, silvery radioactive metallic element.

FOR MORE INFORMATION

Books

Rosinsky, Natalie M. *The Story of the Atomic Bomb: How It Changed the World*. Minneapolis: Compass Point Books, 2010.

Sheinkin, Steve. *Bomb: The Race to Build and Steal the World's Most Dangerous Weapon*. New York: Roaring Brook Press, 2012.

Sullivan, Edward T. *The Ultimate Weapon: The Race to Develop the Atomic Bomb*. New York: Holiday House, 2007.

Websites

The Atomic Heritage Foundation
www.atomicheritage.org

Hiroshima Peace Memorial Museum and Park
www.pcf.city.hiroshima.jp/index_e2.html

The National WWII Museum: For Students
www.nationalww2museum.org/learn/education/for-students

INDEX

About the Author

Angie Smibert is the author of several young adult science fiction novels, including the Memento Nora series, numerous short stories, and several educational titles. She's written about the history and subsequent environmental cleanup of the Manhattan Project sites.